AF487923

Published in the United States of America

Silent Books Publishing, Baltimore, MD

This book was produced in partnership with Silent Books Publishing, a full-service self-publishing company helping authors bring their stories to life.

silentbookspublishing.com

ISBN: 979-8-9911861-6-2

Illustrations and Design by Morgan Elliott

Printed in the United States of America

2026

This Book Belongs To

In Loving Memory of
Paul Devastey

SUPER SAFE

It was a sunny morning at Summit Park Elementary, and Crew couldn't wait to start the day in Ms. Stellar's pre-K class. His backpack was bright blue, and he was grinning from ear to ear.

Crew loved school! Circle time, painting, and especially recess. "The monkey bars are calling my name!" he said to his friends as they lined up to go outside.

Ms. Stellar reminded everyone, "Remember, friends, play safely, take turns, and hold on tight!" Crew nodded quickly. He was too excited to listen for long.

Out on the playground, Crew raced to the monkey bars. "Watch how fast I can go!" he shouted. He climbed high, swung his arms, and felt like a superhero.

But superheroes don't always land perfectly. Crew's hand slipped, and before he knew it! THUMP! He fell to the ground and felt a sharp pain in his arm.

Ms. Stellar ran to him right away. "It's okay, Crew. Don't move your arm. Help is on the way." Crew's eyes filled with tears, but he stayed brave.

At the nurse's office, they called Mom. Mom came right away and took Crew to the doctor. The doctor said Crew's arm was broken and he would need a bright green cast. "Green like the playground grass!" Crew said, trying to smile.

When he came back to school, everyone signed his cast. Ms. Stellar gave him a gold star for being so brave. "I learned my lesson," Crew told his friends. "Superheroes follow safety rules!

Together, the class made a 'Playground Safety Poster.' They wrote: Hold on tight! Take turns! Listen to your teacher! If something looks risky, wait for help!

When Crew sees the monkey bars now, he gives them a brave smile. "Safety powers... activate!" he says, taking his time and holding on tight. The fun doesn't stop, it just gets super safe.

Thank You For Reading!

SUPER Safe

Crew's Playground Lesson

1. Playground
A place at school where kids play outside on swings, slides, and monkey bars.

2. Recess
A time during the school day when kids get to play and have fun outside.

3. Monkey Bars
Bars that kids hold onto and swing across using their hands.

4. Safety
Being careful so you don't get hurt while playing.

5. Rules
Instructions that help everyone stay safe and play fairly.

6. Brave
Being strong and calm, even when something scary happens.

7. Risky
Something that might be dangerous if you are not careful.

8. Doctor
A person who helps take care of you when you are hurt or sick.

9. Cast
A hard cover that protects a broken bone while it heals.

10. Lesson
Something you learn that helps you make better choices next time.

About the Main Character

Crew is energetic, curious, and full of excitement. Sometimes he gets a little too excited, but he is learning the importance of staying safe and following directions from trusted adults.

About the Author

Ty Johnson is Crew's mom and his biggest supporter. She believes that learning about safety should feel calm, loving, and empowering. She wrote this book to help children understand how to stay safe while knowing they are always supported and protected.

Author's Message to Kids

Always stay safe and stay super! Safety is one of the most important rules in life. Even grown-ups have to follow it too. When adults drive cars, they must watch for other cars to keep everyone safe.

Learning about safety early helps protect you as you grow. Always stay super safe, and remember to talk with a trusted adult if something feels scary or confusing.

With love,
Ty Johnson